Mildly self-deprecating, gently humorous, and strongly reinforcing of every American's civic responsibilities, *When the Senate Cared* is a great read. The reader will come away from this book with a sense of having been given a very special tour by a very knowledgeable insider.
—*Richard Baker,* co-editor of *First Among Equals: Outstanding U.S. Senate Leaders in the Twentieth Century*

When the Senate Cared is a fascinating account of Bill Hildenbrand's experiences working for the United States Senate. We shared some of those years, Bill working for the Republican leadership, while I worked for the Democratic leadership. A commitment to responsible governing was shared by the leadership and staff of both parties. *When the Senate Cared* covers many historic issues, including the Vietnam War, opening diplomatic relations with the People's Republic of China, Watergate, the Panama Canal Treaties. Beyond the entertainment value of Bill's stories—there are some very entertaining accounts of life in the Senate—there is a serious message: politics matters, the Senate matters, and congressional leadership is essential to the future of our nation.
—*C. Abbott "Abby" Saffold,* Democratic secretary, United States Senate, 1987–1995 and Democratic Policy Committee, floor staff, 1979–1987

A book not *only* about when the Senate cared—but when Bill Hildenbrand *always* cared! He served two U.S. Senator Simpsons: Dad (Milward) and me. To me, he was one of the honest "old pros" who smoothed my path in early Senate years. Dad always referred to Bill as, "one of nature's noble men." He is that. His memories as jogged here are special reading.
—*Former senator Alan Simpson,* (R) Wyoming

Bill Hildenbrand, the masterful steward-in-chief of the once-formidable and effective United States Senate, reveals for the first time the way the

Senate really was in an earlier time, offering portraits of its leaders and bumblers, disclosing deals that made history, and lamenting the tragic loss of an assembly of great statesmen who governed with wisdom and distinction. A must-read memoir packed with humor and insight, and a valuable critique for all who believe in and care about good government.

—*James Cannon,* former chief of staff for former Senate Majority Leader Howard Baker, and biographer of President Ford

Not since Isaac Bassett's private diaries were discovered about thirty years ago has any steward of the Senate captured the essence of everyday life in the Senate. Bill Hildenbrand's compilation of vignettes from his many years of service to the Senate echo Bassett's observations of the previous century. Isaac Bassett worked in one capacity or another from the 1820s until his death in 1895. About that time Mark Trice was born, and shortly thereafter he came to the Senate as a page and never left. When Trice retired in the 1970s, he was succeeded by Hildenbrand. Collectively these three individuals served more than one hundred fifty years. All three of these men cared deeply about the Senate—"the greatest deliberative body in the world." Moreover, they understood the unique role the Senate performs in our federal system of government. Just as importantly, they understood that the Senate is an aggregation of only one hundred individuals—all equal and fully capable of asserting their individual whims and wishes. They also fully understood the role the Senate performs in protecting the minority from a tyrannical majority, which is the essence of the institution in our system of government. All three men worked for the leadership of the Senate. Hildenbrand was so identified with the Republican leadership of the Senate in his day that the *New York Times* described him as the 101st Senator. Hildenbrand's stories are all the more worth reading because they reflect how the Senate can work when its members

remember to inject comity and trust in their deliberations. I think you will enjoy the book and hearing how things once were and might be again.
—*John Tuck,* former White House aide to President Reagan's chief of staff, (former Senator) Howard Baker

When the Senate Cared

When the Senate Cared

William F. Hildenbrand

iUniverse, Inc.
New York Lincoln Shanghai

When the Senate Cared

iUniverse books may be ordered through booksellers or by contacting:

iUniverse
2021 Pine Lake Road, Suite 100
Lincoln, NE 68512
www.iuniverse.com
1-800-Authors (1-800-288-4677)

Because of the dynamic nature of the Internet, any Web addresses or links contained in this book may have changed since publication and may no longer be valid.

The views expressed in this work are solely those of the author and do not necessarily reflect the views of the publisher, and the publisher hereby disclaims any responsibility for them.

ISBN: 978-0-595-42709-3 (pbk)
ISBN: 978-0-595-69706-9 (cloth)
ISBN: 978-0-595-87039-4 (ebk)

Printed in the United States of America

This book is dedicated to our Senate leaders who served
from 1961 to 1985:

Everett McKinley Dirksen, (R) Illinois
Mike Mansfield, (D) Montana
Hugh Scott, (R) Pennsylvania
Robert Byrd, (D) West Virginia
Howard Baker, (R) Tennessee

To these five Senate statesmen, I owe my career.
It was their leadership and passion for the Senate
that guided us all through those tumultuous times.

Pause for a moment and consider happenings in the United States during
those twenty-five years:

Assassination of a sitting president
Civil Rights Act of 1964
Vietnam War
Resumption of relations with the People's Republic of China
Resignation of a vice president
Senate election of a vice president
Resignation of a president
Return of control of the Panama Canal to the Panamanians

Contents

In Appreciation

My thanks to our fine Senate historian, Dick Baker, and to Associate Historian Don Ritchie for their help in making sure the events were in the right century, even when I was careless. It was a pleasure to "work" with them again. My thanks to my friend, Susan, for her help in turning my gibberish into readable prose. Her support and diligence in the construction of this manuscript are greatly appreciated. And most of all, my thanks to my wife, Shirley, for her willingness to read and criticize the gibberish all over again.

Foreword

Reading Bill Hildenbrand's manuscript brings to mind more than good memories for me. It is a reminder that those who have dedicated themselves to nurturing and sustaining the principles of representative government are worthy of our sincerest praise.

In this memoir one can find a refreshing sense of good humor injected into some of the most important episodes of our national history. For instance, in his description of his argument with Chinese officials during a late night confrontation over the use by a Senate delegation of its U.S. Air Force plane for travel among cities in country, the author fails to take credit for personally altering a Chinese national policy that had perplexed career officials in the United States for years.

On other pages, we are reminded of the personality and tenacity involved in winning and losing intramural Senate leadership elections and in the passage of major legislation that has shaped our history. In a word, you can describe this book as "refreshing," and be glad that our distinguished, good friend, the former Secretary of the United States Senate, took the time to write it.

—Senator Thad Cochran, (R) Mississippi

Preface

This book recounts various leadership races in the U.S. Senate and also relates humorous incidents that occurred on Congressional Delegation (Codel) trips in various foreign lands.

As many of you are aware, the Congress, for a number of years, took unfair criticism from the media for foreign trips labeled as "junkets"—trips to exotic places with no legislative or administrative purposes—and on taxpayers' money. Were there such trips? Of course, but not nearly as many as the press would have you believe. In my more than twenty-five years in the Senate, I have found that the taxpayers more than got their money's worth in sound legislative proposals that made our country stand tall throughout the world, such as the Panama Canal Treaty discussed in the book.

I hope you find humor in my musings about the foreign trips. Although almost unbelievable, they really are true stories—even though you might say, "Yeah, right!"

Hell No, We Won't Go

The year was 1966. The war in Vietnam continued, and the members of Congress were most unhappy. They took to the floor on an almost non-stop basis to complain bitterly about what they considered to be McNamara's war, orchestrated by Robert McNamara, President Lyndon Johnson's secretary of defense. These were not the only voices being raised against the Vietnam War. These, however, were the only ones vocalizing their opposition every day on the Senate floor.

The Democratic group was made up Senator Wayne Morse of Oregon, Senator Ernest Gruening of Arkansas, and Senator George McGovern of South Dakota. Senator Morse was considered a maverick. Elected to the Senate as a Republican in 1944, he had opposed Ike Eisenhower's plan in 1952 to name Richard Nixon as his vice president and became an Independent, which caused him not to have a seat on the Senate floor. When he appeared for his swearing in, he brought with him a folding chair and seated himself in the middle aisle between the Democrats and Republicans. He soon realized that as an Independent he would not get a committee assignment and could not pursue his legislative issues, and, therefore, he became a Democrat. In 1953, he set the Senate record for continuous speech by not yielding the floor for twenty-two hours and six minutes.

Senator Gruening had been territorial governor of Alaska, and when statehood came to Alaska in 1959, he was named one of the two senators to represent the forty-ninth state. Always an opponent of the Vietnam War, he was one of two senators to vote against the Tonkin Gulf Resolution to extend the war; Senator Morse cast the other vote.

McGovern's distinction, of course, would be to run as the Democrat's presidential nominee to oppose Richard Nixon in 1972. It was not a highlight of his career—he lost by the largest landslide in U.S. political history.

1

Thirsty or Not,
Don't Reach for a Glass

So, with the war still raging, protestors were out in force, even sitting in the halls outside the Senate chamber, down the corridor, and into the minority leader's office. Members had to step over them to get in to vote. At about seven o'clock one evening, I spoke with the group's leader and asked him to have the group leave so I could close the office, stating that I would otherwise have to call the police. They did not comply, so I had them removed.

Meanwhile, on the floor, Senators Morse, Gruening, and McGovern continued their nightly harangue against Johnson's administration. Senator Morse had the floor and, as usual, was in good voice. The presiding officer was Maryland's Democratic senator, Daniel Brewster, who was seeking reelection and had a major fundraiser downtown that evening. Under Senate rules, the majority party must preside and the Democratic leadership staff was trying feverishly to find a stand-in. It got later and later, and the senator from Oregon kept talking and talking.

Also under Senate rules, a member cannot be taken off the floor while speaking unless and until he stops talking. Senator Morse made a critical error when he stopped for a split second to reach for a glass of water. Before he could touch his glass, the gavel banged, and Senator Brewster said, "The Senate stands adjourned," leaving a sputtering Morse still wanting to speak.

Senate rules specify that once the gavel falls and adjournment is announced, there is no way to get the Senate back into session until noon the next day. A visibly upset Morse rushed from the chamber to Majority Leader Mike Mansfield's office to relate just what had happened to him. Mansfield calmed Senator Morse down and alerted the Democratic staff to put out a hotline informing all that the Senate would convene in Executive Session the next day at noon. Behind closed doors and without staff present, the senators went back and forth for two hours until they agreed that no move to adjourn would be recognized unless made by the leadership. Whew! Things quieted down for a while with that. (By the way, Senator Brewster won his reelection.)

Just Say No—I Owe You One

It was campaign time for others as well: my boss, Senator Caleb Boggs of Delaware, was seeking reelection to the Senate on the Republican side. Boggs had been a three-term congressman from 1947 to 1953 and had retired to run for governor in 1954. The year for school desegregation, an issue not too popular in Delaware's southern three counties, had been 1953. So in 1954, it made sense that the Republican State Committee had misgivings about Boggs's electability. Senator Boggs, when governor, had supported the Supreme Court decision on school desegregation, and the three southern counties in Delaware opposed the decision. So, the politicians in the Republican Party thought that Boggs would lose too many votes in those lower two counties to be elected. Also, Boggs's opponent was a resident of one of those counties. At the Nominating Convention in Dover, a committee rep from a northern county convinced the delegates of Boggs's chances, and she was right: he was elected and served until he decided to run again for the Senate.

The 1959 Senate race was the fourth time Boggs faced the Delaware voters. In that race he had had labor support, which he would not have in 1966. Labor's 1959 support for Boggs was more accurately described as, "opposition to Senator Frear," but Senator Boggs was not on labor's reelection list for 1966. Republican office holders in Delaware were not pro-labor.

One afternoon in the middle of the 1966 reelection campaign, Senator Boggs was sitting at his desk on the Senate floor when Senator Bobby Kennedy ((D) New York) entered the chamber. The room's configuration required Kennedy to go behind Senator Boggs to get to his seat on the Democratic side. He paused as he passed Boggs, pulled out a chair, and sat down. The two engaged in a calm discussion until Kennedy threw up his hands, got up, pushed back the chair, and went to his desk. Of course, nosy me, who had witnessed this exchange, rushed over to see what it was all about.

Boggs said, "Well, he has a small political problem, although it's not unsolvable." The Democratic Party in Delaware was pulling all the strings and turning all the screws to get Kennedy to come to a fundraiser in Delaware for Boggs's opponent, who just happened to be the chief justice of the State Supreme Court. I had a sinking feeling when I pictured all that money going into our opponent's pockets to buy more campaign ads and television time—money that I knew we could not match. Boggs, being the gracious man he was, had told Kennedy simply, "Well, Bobby, you have to do what you think is right and what you are comfortable with. You and I have been friends and we will still be friends." He said Kennedy looked at him for a few moments and then said, "Hell, Cale, I don't have time to go to Delaware; I've got too much on my plate. I'm just going to tell them no." Boggs said, "Well, it's up to you, Bobby." That's when Kennedy had left for his own desk. So much for this tough partisan who was pictured as taking no prisoners—it was quite a favor he did for Boggs, and we thanked him. Boggs was reelected that year, too.

The Republicans' Storyteller

Thomas Kuchel, the Republican whip, was not as fortunate as Boggs had been. Senator Kuchel of California liked to amuse his colleagues with funny stories; he was the Republicans' storyteller. One day in the back of the chamber, he was discussing a construction bill, the so-called "Bill with Projects for Everybody." Kuchel said that the debate reminded him of a time when, as a member of the California legislature, they too had a public works bill before them—a pork-barrel bill full of state bridges, buildings, and roads to nowhere for each senator. He said the speaker was announcing the bill's overview and turned to Representative Gonzalez and said, "You'll be happy to know that we are going to build a bridge across the Pima River." Representative Gonzalez paid no attention. The Speaker said, "I'm sorry, Representative, did you not hear me? We are going to build a bridge across the Pima River." With that, Gonzalez got up and said, "I heard, Mr. Speaker. But we don't need a bridge; I can pee halfway across the Pima River." The Speaker shouted, "You're out of order! You're out of order!" to which Representative Gonzalez replied, "I know. If I was in order I could pee *all* the way across the Pima River!"

That was the Tom Kuchel we knew—the storyteller. Unfortunately, he lost in that '66 election to California educator Max Rafferty. The Republicans lost not only their storyteller, but also the number-two man in their leadership.

Keystoner versus Cornhusker—Race for the Whip

After Senator Kuchel's defeat left a vacancy, Senator Dirksen ((R) Illinois) wasted no time in letting his colleagues know that he was supporting Senator Roman Hruska of Nebraska to fill the whip position. That endorsement sent chills through the moderate wing of the party—it was actually a tizzy—led by Clifford Case of New Jersey, Jacob Javits of New York, and John Sherman Cooper of Kentucky. They knew that if Hruska were elected, they would be completely out of the ball game; they'd be lucky to even know what day the Senate would be called to session! In searching around for a moderate to pull into a run against Hruska, they settled on the pipe-smoking, urbane, and articulate senator from Pennsylvania by the name of Hugh Scott. He had all the right seasoning. He had been a House member, had authored the book *Come to the Party*, had helped Eisenhower defeat Taft in the 1952 Nominating Convention, and was generally well respected in the Senate. The conservative Republican senators were also concerned, but for a different reason than the moderates. The conservatives realized that if Hruska were elected whip and something happened to Minority Leader Dirksen, Hruska would become the leader until the conference chairman called a new election and all Republican members could seek the position. However, the possibility of Scott's rise under such circumstances was of no concern to conservative Republicans, because they had the votes to defeat him.

So the lines were drawn for the whip contest, Cornhusker versus Keystoner. As soon as Scott agreed to run, he named a neighbor and old friend, my boss, Senator Boggs, to be his campaign manager. Boggs enjoyed respect among the conservatives, even though he was an avowed moderate. Scott told all his supporters that a vote would be counted in his column when he had spoken personally to the senator. Scott estimated he would need twenty-four votes to be successful. The vote would be on the day of convening, which did not allow much time to contact the members, what with Santa Claus just around the corner. God love Graham Bell for making it possible to talk to a lot of members who had gone back to their home states—Scott called them all. On the day of the vote, Scott told his supporters he had twenty-four committed votes. The secret ballot vote was 24–20, much to the chagrin of Senator Dirksen and Hruska's supporters.

Whippin' Up

With Senator Scott elected as whip, maybe I should enlighten the reader as to what a whip does. Whips, when directed by the leader, poll the party's members to determine their positions on legislation or on decisions being made by the leadership. Various methods are employed by the whip and his staff. Senator Scott used the face-to-face method, the one he used in his race against Hruska and Baker. The method of talking directly to the member had served him well, so he continued it. Other whips utilized committee chairmen, a ranking member, or their own staff to poll the members. Using one's own staff is by far the most risky one for getting an accurate count. A staff member talks to another staff member and eventually gets the senators' positions—maybe. Leadership usually does not like or put a lot of faith in the count if this method is used. Most counts are important because their purpose is to ascertain likely passage or defeat of a legislative matter, and also to learn which members need some persuading.

For example, the importance of a whip check is clear in an example of a situation when it was obvious that things for President Nixon were not going well. Chairman Peter Rodino and his judiciary committee colleagues were preparing Articles of Impeachment. Before those articles found their way to the Senate, Senator Scott said that our members needed to know how a trial would play out. Hence, a whip check was conducted. The numbers disturbed Senator Scott, as it was evident that a vote for impeachment would carry. These numbers were discussed at the policy luncheon that directed Senators Goldwater and Scott to meet with the president and discuss resignation. Without those numbers, it is unlikely that President Nixon would have stepped down. It would have been hard for him to believe that so many of his friends had left the field. And that is the whip's duty—it's not always pleasant, but whips are a dramatic and effective tool.

Scott Takes the Lead

Scott, like the good soldier he was, sat in his new whip office waiting to be instructed what to do next. I, on the other hand, had decided I wanted to make a change. On the floor, I had been a friend of Senator Scott for some time. My original roots were in Pennsylvania, and I knew a lot about that state. I offered Scott my counsel about pending legislation and potential impacts on Pennsylvania. After Scott was elected whip, I became aware of my own uncertainty about what Boggs was going to do about the 1972 election, or how that decision would affect me.

One evening, I attended a welcome reception for newly elected Senator Mac Mathias of Maryland. Directly ahead of me in line was Gene Cowan, Senator Scott's administrative assistant. Cowan asked if I knew of anyone who might like to be administrative assistant to the newly elected whip and, without hesitation, I suggested myself. He thought it was a great idea, but advised that Scott and Boggs should discuss my shift in allegiance. So I asked Boggs to relieve me of my duties so that I could bid for a position with Senator Scott. Boggs, always the gentleman, encouraged me to apply for the position. I did, and I was appointed by Scott.

This was a rather difficult time for Senator Scott because Senator Dirksen was not a bit happy with his election. The staffers around him, under Mark Trice, secretary of the minority, and his assistant, Billy Brownrigg, were not fans of Scott, and it was hard to find out what exactly was going to happen on the floor. The floor staff had all been appointed by Senator Dirksen, and they were all conservatives. Senator Scott's liberal leanings were too much for them, so they did not help at all.

Senator Dirksen was hospitalized in April 1969. Senate Republican rules mandated that when the leader is incapacitated, the whip becomes the temporary leader, so Scott was now at the leadership of the Republicans. Previously, Scott had determined that the concept of regional whips was a grand idea; this was now his chance to put the idea into action! Of course, someone called Dirksen in the hospital and told him what Scott was about to do. Dirksen immediately called Scott and said, "No you're not. There are going to be no regional whips. Leadership stands the way that it is." This call put an end to Scott's regional whip idea.

Later, during discussion of a military bill, Senator Scott announced on the floor that he had just talked to the administration and learned that they supported an amendment to that bill. Upon hearing this, the ranking minority member of the Armed Services Committee, John Tower of Texas (who was the first conservative Republican senator from Texas), came out of the Republican cloakroom in quite a hurry. Hearing what Scott had announced, he immediately got the floor and contradicted Scott; Tower said that *he* had just talked with the administration, and they did *not* support this bill and, in fact, they urged every Republican member to vote against it. This is exactly what happened—just one of the many things that Scott had to face as a whip who really was neither the leader's favorite nor, as it turned out, a favorite of most of the Republican floor staff. In 1969, the Senate for the first time decided to take advantage of a law that had been passed a few years earlier that permitted the Senate to recess beginning on the first Saturday following August 1st and ending the Tuesday following Labor Day. This was a good thing from our standpoint because it gave us at least a month to not have to fight with the Dirksen people about who the leader was or was not.

Unfortunately, on the Sunday before Labor Day, Senator Dirksen passed away, and on the Tuesday following Labor Day, Senator Scott called his colleagues, supporters, and staff together and told them that until Senator Dirksen had been laid to rest, there would be no discussion of his possible successor. Indeed, it wasn't until after the senator's funeral, when the members had returned, that Senator Scott revealed that he would seek the leader's position. However, unbeknownst to us (and also to Senator Howard Baker himself), a Baker staff person went to see Senator Robert Packwood of Oregon that Tuesday to inform him that Senator Baker had indicated that he was going to seek his father-in-law's position as the leader. The members immediately recognized the impropriety of this and, in fact, one member from Idaho clipped a news article from an Oregon paper where Packwood had gone on record with Baker's intentions. The senator carried it around in his pocket until the leadership conference race was decided, showing it to all the other senators.

Conference Chairman Margaret Chase Smith of Maine decreed that the conference would meet September 24th to elect a new leader. By that time, in addition to Senator Scott announcing, so too had Senator Baker, Senator Hruska of whip-race fame, and Jack Miller of Iowa. Senator Scott campaigned as he had previously, visiting with each member, looking him in the eye, and getting a decision as to whether the member would support him or support Baker, Hruska, or Miller. Senator Scott, counting up his checkmarks, determined that he had twenty-four sure votes—sufficient to be elected leader. And in fact, as it turned out, the announced vote was Scott 24, Baker 19—we had our new leader.

The afternoon session was to elect a whip. The contestants in that campaign were Senator Baker, who had indicated previously that he would run if he was not elected leader, Michigan's Senator Bob Griffin, Senator Ted Stevens of Alaska, and again Jack Miller, the senator from Iowa. That vote was taken, and Senator Griffin of Michigan was victorious and became the whip to Senator Scott. Scott's memories of his own trials and tribulations as whip were fresh in his mind, and he immediately set about including his new whip in the leadership councils.

Sensitive to Baker's two lost races in the same day, Scott told our staff that if there were anything that we could do to help, particularly in Baker's reelection efforts in Tennessee, we ought to do it. Congress had recently formed a new Joint Committee on Atomic Energy, and since there were a large number of nuclear facilities in Tennessee, Scott thought to appoint Baker to it.

Senate business went along swimmingly with Senator Scott as the new leader. But in January 1971, Baker again announced that he was going to seek the leader position. So it was back to campaigning again, and in early January a conference was called to elect, or reelect, Senator Scott as the leader. Somebody somewhere wanted Scott out of the leadership—and we identified that somebody as President Nixon's chief of staff, H. R. Haldeman. He was doing what he did best—protecting the President's back. Senator Scott had a long and friendly relationship with Nixon through the years, but they did not agree politically; in most cases, Nixon's positions were much more conservative than Scott's.

Senator Scott performed his usual campaign survey and determined that when they went to the conference that morning, he still had the twenty-four votes that he had had previously. The results? Exactly as predicted: Scott 24, Baker 20. Baker's votes included Senator John Sherman Cooper, who thoughtfully came to Scott to tell him that Baker was a relative and he did not feel he could vote against him. Again, Scott thanked him for the heads-up. Once again, Senator Scott wanted to soften the sting of defeat for Baker, and in February 1973 he appointed him the ranking member of the Senate Watergate Committee.

One from Column A and One from Column B

Prior to President Nixon turning his attention to second-term reelection in 1972, he and Secretary of State Henry Kissinger made an important trip. For the first time since 1948, the United States was going to attempt to normalize relations with the People's Republic of China—the duo was headed for Beijing. There had been no back-and-forth between the two countries for almost twenty-five years, since the ascension to power of Chairman Mao Zedong and, as the positives in Nixon's legacy confirm, the trip and the dialogue it opened between the United States and China are heralded as tremendous successes.

Upon his return home, the president told the country that more diplomatic exchanges were to follow. He contacted Senate Majority Leader Mike Mansfield and Senate Minority Leader Hugh Scott to inform them that Premier Chou En-lai had suggested that the two senators spearhead such diplomatic exchanges with a near-future visit to China. President Nixon agreed that this was a good idea and committed administration resources to assist the two leaders in their trip. Senators Mansfield and Scott contacted designated unofficial representatives of the People's Republic to work out details about trip dates and length of stay in the People's Republic. Once we reached China, other details were revealed to us with little notice, which continued throughout the trip.

The U.S. delegation was to be small. Senator Mansfield chose Frank Valeo, then secretary of the Senate, his personal secretary Salpee Sahagan, and Bob Dockery, an expert on the Senate Foreign Relations Committee. Senator Scott chose Martin Hamburger, his administrative assistant in the Pennsylvania office, and me. We made many preparations for our eventful journey and in late March, 1972, we flew off to Hawaii, where we overnighted before the next day's journey to Guam—Mansfield wanted the delegation to get a good night's rest there before landing on People's Republic soil. However, the good night's rest was not possible because Admiral John McCain, commander of the Pacific fleet (and father of present-day Senator John McCain), greeted us with news that President Nixon had just ordered an escalation of the bombing in Vietnam to include Haiphong Harbor, after the breakdown of the Paris peace talks. Mansfield was visibly upset by this news and puzzled aloud as to whether the trip could continue in the face of this event—perhaps it would be best to return to the United States. McCain and Scott prevailed upon Mansfield to delay his decision until morning, which he did. The next morning, with trepidation among the entire delegation, Senator Mansfield announced that the trip would go as scheduled and that we would leave later that day for Shanghai—which is exactly what we did.

Shanghai Revolutionary Committee leaders met us upon arrival, and we were given the ceremonial cup of tea—the first of many ceremonial cups of tea to come. Throughout this trip, we were forever "being informed" of our pending next activity—but the explanations were of events so imminent it felt like they were just descriptions of the present!

First up, we were "informed" that the military plane that had transported us thus far could go no further and would be sent out of China. We were to unload our belongings. Sitting on the tarmac was a British viscount carrying the name of China Airlines, and we were "informed" that it would be our transport for the duration of our stay in the People's Republic of China. A pilot, copilot, and two Chinese stewards were our hosts for the sixteen days that we were in country.

We flew into the airport in Beijing and motored along the sides of the roads past people who waved at us—probably because we gave the appearance of a formal parade. I really believe they had no more idea of who we were than the man in the moon; they just believed we certainly must be important, and so they waved.

We arrived at a compound that was completely walled in and fronted by iron gates—our home for the entire stay. The compound had been diplomatic headquarters for the East German contingent and was made up of a number of separate houses to which we were assigned, two to a house. Senators Mansfield and Scott each had their own accommodations. Chinese assistants took care of our housekeeping needs.

We settled in, showered, were informed where to leave our dirty clothes, and were off to dinner within the compound—typical American fare of steak, potatoes, and vegetables plus the ever-present cup of tea. Our hosts were members of the Foreign Policy Institute, who throughout the trip did most of the "informing" of what our itinerary's next line item was. So ... after dinner we learned that we *would learn* at breakfast the next day what that day's schedule would include!

As Senator Scott was an expert in Chinese culture, art, and history, his interests led him (to lead us) in pursuit of what was beyond the compound wall. But when we reached the iron gates, two soldiers politely informed us that we were not permitted outside. Although we intellectually knew we were on a controlled regimen in a controlled land, it nevertheless was alarming to be in the moment of realizing limitations put on us by a foreign Communist regime and to be cut off from our familiar other world. We hid our fear and went to bed. That was the end of our first night in Beijing!

Marching music at six the next morning awakened us—it was the accompaniment to customary Chinese morning exercises! Two houseboys arrived with tea and coffee and we were off to more American fare—bacon, eggs, toast, and more information! The foreign policy reps told us we were going to visit a Chinese hospital and witness a caesarian delivery during which only acupuncture would be used as an anesthetic. We were fascinated. (Of course, maybe we would have been fascinated to observe a caesarian in the United States using conventional anesthetics.) At the hospital, we ascended to a balcony and viewed the operating room below. One acupuncture needle was placed in the pregnant woman's abdomen on her right side and another on the left side. One needle each was placed also in the top of each leg. With preparation completed, the operation was to proceed—with the patient fully conscious. Soon we heard the cry of a newborn. We Americans exchanged looks of wonderment at what we had just witnessed.

From the hospital, we were taken to see the enormously impressive Summer Palace and returned to our residences where we were informed that the premier had invited us for dinner at the Great Hall at 7:00. We arrived at the Great Hall and, I must admit, were greatly impressed to witness Premier Chou En-lai and his delegation stride down a corridor towards us. Chou En-lai was a monumental world figure about whom we had read so much—and here he was in the flesh. The premier welcomed us, and Senators Mansfield and Scott offered greetings in return.

At the premier's invitation following dinner, both senators and select staff met with him in a room furnished with large, overstuffed chairs separated by tables with the ceremonial tea on each one. The premier opened conversation with a question to Scott: "Senator, did you bring a copy of your book?" Senator Scott had recently completed writing *The Golden Age of Chinese Art*. Quite complimented but somewhat embarrassed, Senator Scott confessed that he had not brought a copy, but promised at his earliest opportunity to forward one to the premier.

Discussion then turned to issues about World War II and China's participation. Since both Mansfield and Scott had served in the war, it was of interest to them to see how the Chinese looked upon Japanese entrance into the war. The premier indicated that this war was not a case of the people versus the people, but rather that their fight was with the government of Japan and certainly not the people.

After more civilities, it was time to say good night, and back to the residences we went. We again learned the next day's itinerary at breakfast—this time the scheduled event was to meet with experts from the Foreign Policy Institute. Discussions focused on emerging Chinese engagement with the nations of the world and delineating their aspirations. Our delegation indicated what our intentions might be, especially regarding possible trade ramifications. We broke for lunch and resumed these discussions in the afternoon.

The next day's breakfast announcement informed us that we would be off to see the Great Wall. What an awesome sight that stretched for miles. We were allowed to walk the wall and climb up to the parapets strung all along it. Do you think that is what President Bush has in mind for the border between Mexico and the United States?

When we returned to our residences after that trip, we learned that we would attend an official dinner at the Great Hall hosted by the leaders of the Foreign Policy Institute. Seated at dining tables with cuisine we could not quite identify, we enjoyed a rather delicious meal.

The next morning we departed for West Lake and Hangzhou, where President Nixon had planted some trees alongside the lake as a gesture of friendship with the Chinese. We were met there by leaders of the Hangzhou Revolutionary Committee and shared a very restful lunch in a most beautiful setting. Hangzhou is one of two vacation cities for Chinese diplomats at home on rest and relaxation time following foreign assignments. It truly is a most tranquil place.

The next day we visited a very new Chinese discovery—an archeological find of life-size terra-cotta warriors "protecting" the mausoleum of China's first emperor. Believed to have been constructed sometime earlier than 200 BC, it is among China's proudest attractions; it was truly quite a sight. More such discoveries have been made in the same vicinity, and they, too, are among the wonders of China.

Prior to our departure for Shanghai the next morning, Senator Scott decided to try one more time to see any part of Beijing that he could, so we went to the gates and, lo and behold, two smiling Chinese soldiers opened them and let us out! As we strode down the small street, we were immediately surrounded by curious citizenry wondering who we were and what were we doing there. We came to a small side street that had a lot of small shops. Scott, of course, wanted to see what might be for sale, so we entered. The crowd outside soon grew quite large. The staff of the Foreign Policy Institute had learned we were on the streets, but, not knowing exactly where, they were concerned and came looking. Needless to say, when they saw the crowd outside the store, they knew they had found something other than a closeout sale. They caught up with us in the store and very politely asked us to return with them.

Aboard China Airlines the next morning, we departed for Shanghai where we were again met by the leaders of the Shanghai Revolutionary

Committee and again enjoyed the ceremonial pot of tea. We toured the city and went out on the Yangtze River to see some of the World War II fortifications constructed to keep the Japanese from getting into the river and into Shanghai. They were quite elaborate and very effective. In Shanghai, we went to see a small plant that manufactured small wooden elephants. It may be of some interest to note that the craftsmen used no modern vises to hold their wood in place while carving these elephants. Rather, at each desk, under the leg and up the side was a leather strap that went over the piece of wood and then down on the other side to be locked again under the leg. Of course, they carved many other items as well, but we were struck by the primitive means used to do such carvings.

The next day we had a final meeting with Foreign Policy Institute representatives and on the day after, we left for the border—via China Airlines, of course—stopping overnight in Canton. From there via train, we reached the border crossing between the People's Republic of China and Hong Kong. There were many, many emotional good-byes at the border, as one can imagine. The two delegations had been together for sixteen days during which many thoughts, histories, and cultural nuances had been exchanged. The women, especially, had shared many secrets of the ways of the western and ancient worlds. There were many red eyes in each delegation. Then it was time to leave.

As we started across the bridge, we could see the U.S. ambassador to British Hong Kong and Hong Kong's mayor in the distance. Just as our first visit to the Great Hall was awesome, it was overwhelmingly awesome to feel that we were now, in fact, walking to freedom.

We spent two days in Hong Kong before returning to the States. While there, Senator Scott found a copy of *The Golden Age of Chinese Art*, inscribed it, and promptly sent it via the embassy to Premier Chou En-lai.

It flies just like ours!

The former East German Embassy.

Exchange of views with Premier Chou En-lai.

The U.S. delegation's home in China
for our sixteen-day trip in 1972.

The Great Wall of China.

You'd think they'd have chairs.

Terra-cotta soldiers.

Republican elephants.

The Mansfield-Scott delegation departs Beijing.

They Couldn't Rob Their Kids' Piggy Banks

With the China trip behind us, attention now focused on the upcoming presidential election in November 1972. During the summer, a few members of the Committee to Re-elect the President decided that they really needed additional information about what the Democrats were planning, what kind of attacks they would have against the president, and what issues they would bring up. One of them decided that a way to find this information would be to get into the Democratic National Committee Headquarters. So a little band of banditos snuck in the back door of the Watergate Hotel late one night and into the suite of the headquarters. However, their undoing came because they Scotch-taped the latch on their exit door so that it would not lock. Of course, the security guard, making his rounds, saw the taped door, immediately knew that someone had entered the hotel, and immediately called the police. When the banditos completed their work and were about to leave, they were met with a contingent of Washington DC police and were arrested.

This caused quite a furor. The Democrats wanted to know if President Nixon had prior knowledge of the plan to break-in to the headquarters, and whether he did, in fact, authorize the break-in. Nixon said he had no knowledge of the plan and had not authorized it. Nixon's reply did not satisfy Senate Democrats, who created a Watergate Committee in February 1973; the House impeachment inquiry under Peter Rodino got underway a year later.

Based on information that unfolded at those hearings, the possibility of voting Articles of Impeachment became increasingly apparent. The president, in attempting to forestall such action, named a special prosecutor to undertake an investigation of exactly what had happened and who was responsible for it. He named former Secretary of Health, Education, and Welfare Elliott Richardson as the special counsel, who went about his assigned duties of investigating what had transpired in the Watergate break-in.

At the same time, the House hearings droned on. Senator Mansfield met with Senator Scott to discuss that if the House were to vote Articles of Impeachment, the Senate would become the court of last resort, whose evidence would be solely the work of the House Judiciary Committee. Therefore, Mansfield proposed that the Senate form a Special Watergate Committee to begin its own investigation. He named Sam Ervin of North Carolina to be chairman of that committee. Senator Scott had become increasingly respectful of the senator from Tennessee, Howard Baker, for his knowledge and elegance, and so named him as vice chairman. Senator Scott had been similarly impressed by a newly elected senator from Connecticut, Lowell Weicker, and he too was named to the committee.

When Senator Scott looked at the makeup of the committee, he realized that there was no one on it who would be carrying the banner for the president of the United States. With that in mind, he named an arch conservative from Florida, Senator Ed Gurney, whose appointment completed the eight-member Watergate Committee. Hearings then commenced. Incidentally, the minority counsel appointed by Senator Baker was Fred Thompson, also a Tennessean, who went on to enjoy fame as an actor, then served as a U.S. senator from 1994 to 2003 and, at this writing, is making a bid for the presidency.

As hearings proceeded, the Watergate Committee was unexpectedly confronted with the testimony that there was an audio taping system in the White House where all conversations were recorded and housed. This caused great consternation in the Senate and the House of Representatives, which immediately called for a release of the tapes. To prevent their release, President Nixon immediately claimed executive privilege; the House responded with a threat to go to court to obtain their release. In an attempt to forestall legal action, President Nixon began to release portions of the tapes that he said would have a bearing on the House investigation. His action did not satisfy the House. Concurrent to all this, President

Nixon suddenly fired Special Investigator Archibald Cox in what is known as the Saturday Night Massacre, as he could not keep Cox from going too far afield. Nixon decided the best way to stop Cox was to fire him—a typical Nixonian tactic. In response, Attorney General Elliot Richardson and Deputy Attorney General William Ruckelshaus resigned. These events caused even more consternation on Capitol Hill.

During all of this, President Nixon was continuing to release tidbits from the tapes and in early December, Chief of Staff Alexander Haig showed up at Senator Scott's house with a document that he said would clearly vindicate the president of any wrongdoing. So Senator Scott, who had been supportive of the president, kept the document for review at the beginning of 1974. His review revealed that the document was not complete; parts of it had been removed. With that knowledge, Senator Scott announced the end of his support for the president. He was not going to be misled any longer.

The Week That Was

Senator Scott met with members of the Republican leadership to discuss exactly where they stood in terms of impeachment if the House voted Articles; what kind of support President Nixon could expect to have at a Senate trial. The differing views among the Republican members caused Senator Scott to conduct a "whip check," the poll taken to determine where each stands on an issue at hand. The questions were very simple. "Do you support the president or do you oppose him? Would you vote for or against conviction?" Senator Scott was taken aback by the results, which indicated that there were at most perhaps fifteen Republicans who would vote in Nixon's favor—a count that could not save the beleaguered president.

Traditionally, for more years than I care to remember, Republican members meet once a week at their so-called "Tuesday luncheon." Also traditionally, the vice president—when he is a Republican—has always been invited to attend those Republican luncheons. At the Tuesday luncheon following Scott's whip check, the only issue anyone wished to discuss was the possibility of impeaching Nixon. Discussions went back and forth throughout the room: What should be done? What shouldn't be done? How it should be done? Should the president resign?

Not long into the debate, Vice President Gerald Ford rose and asked to be excused. He said he didn't believe that he should be present while this discussion continued and stated that he was a little uncomfortable being there. Ford, of course, would have been the direct beneficiary of Nixon's removal from office.

A heated debate continued until finally Barry Goldwater got up and said, "Well, I just have one thing to say. This president has lied to me for the last time." As Goldwater was very well respected, his words carried a lot of weight with the Tuesday luncheon membership, which decided that the president ought to resign; Nixon didn't have enough support to withstand conviction on impeachment charges.

It was agreed that Senators Goldwater and Scott should arrange an audience with President Nixon to convey the Senate's lack of support and to recommend that he resign in order to save the country and the Senate from a long, drawn-out trial. Following their meeting in the Oval Office, the senators reported that Nixon listened very intently to their message and replied, saying, "I'll tell you what. I really have to talk to Pat and the family about this matter, as serious as this one is, and so I will do that this evening and have an answer for you tomorrow morning." The next morning, President Nixon announced that on Thursday at noon he would resign the presidency, and that Vice President Gerry Ford would be sworn in to replace him. And that is exactly what happened.

President Nixon and his family went by helicopter to Andrews Air Force Base where, for the last time, they boarded Air Force One and were taken to their home in California.

There Must Be Somebody Out There Who Can Spell "Conservative" (Not Me)

The year is 1974. President Nixon has resigned, Gerry Ford has been sworn in as president, and there are congressional elections coming up in November. Early in December, Senator Scott received a letter from Mark Trice, the secretary of the minority, advising that he was resigning his post at the end of the year. I had been working in the Senate since 1961 and realized that if I did not attempt to succeed Trice, then I was already sitting on the top rung on my Senate career. I asked Senator Scott about the position, and he encouraged me to go for it, stating he would support me. I sent out letters to the minority party members indicating that I was seeking the post and asking them for their support. When the Senate convened in January, the conference chairman scheduled an election.

The day dawned early and the meeting of the members was set for ten o'clock, at which time they were to elect a new secretary. I had no announced opposition at the time the meeting was called to order. I wasn't present at the meeting, of course—I waited out its lengthy duration in the majority leader's office.

A break in my waiting came with the appearance of the senator from Kansas, James Pearson, at the office entrance. Approaching my desk, he said, "Hildenbrand, you're the only person I've ever known who lost a one-man race." The conference had decided to look around to see if they could find a possible opponent and have another election! A career dead-end flashed before my eyes.

Next to arrive at the office where I was waiting were the two who informally constituted a personnel committee: Senators Howard Baker and Roman Hruska.

"Look," Baker told Hruska, "we should go back in there, elect Hildenbrand and be done with it. I thought Baker's position was a mighty fine one, and succinctly stated so. Hruska didn't want to hear that, but his problem was that I had been with Senator Scott for so long, and Senator Boggs before that. It was evident (to him) that I was not the strong conservative that some would have liked to become Trice's replacement.

I had at this time spent almost fifteen years in the Senate, and all but four of them were in a leadership position. I had managed the floor for Senator Scott and was employed by Senator Boggs before that. In both instances, those two gentlemen were what we used to term "Eisenhower Republicans." An Eisenhower Republican was simply one who was conservative with the people's money and liberal about their needs. The Republican side of the Senate was mostly conservative, and they would not have wanted their party secretary to have political views not shared by the members. I would have been less conservative with your money in order to better fund liberal programs.

In any case, Baker's threat didn't have to be acted upon, as the conference reconvened late that morning, took another vote, and elected me secretary of the minority. (Whew! My career was reinstated, despite being the first and only person to lose a one-man race.) I assumed the office immediately, and for six years acted as their voice on the Senate floor. Most of the staff, that was now my staff, were conservatives and, as a matter of fact, had been employed by Trice. I remained as secretary until 1980, when the Senate became Republican-controlled. At that time I was elected secretary of the Senate.

Senate Bids Good-bye to Two Elder Statesmen

We lost our two leaders in 1976 as Senators Mansfield and Scott retired from the Senate and resigned their party positions. In the next year, the parties elected new leadership—Senator Robert Byrd of West Virginia for the Democrats and Senator Howard Baker of Tennessee for the Republicans. For Senator Baker, it turned out that the third time was the charm. But as the new leadership took over, we also had a new person in the White House, former governor Jimmy Carter of Georgia. As Carter was a Democrat, it became difficult for Senator Baker to keep the members of his party in line in trying to help the president get some of his legislation enacted.

The difference between the majority and minority leaders cannot be more clear than if I relate a small story about Senator Baker's attempt to procure a U.S. Air Force plane to go for a trip to the Soviet Union. In the beginning, the Defense Department said that Baker's request was fine, and they would take care of it. But obviously, someone in the White House did not want to see Senator Baker flying around the world on a United States Air Force plane. As a result, before we ever took off, we found out that we didn't have any plane to take off in. The Defense Department had changed its mind and said, "Sorry, we don't have any planes available."

In the press, there continued to be discussions about foreign travel, which the media had dubbed "junkets." In some cases, that was really what they were—nonessential, wasteful trips. But by and large, the congressional trips that were taken did accomplish what they set out to, which was gather information from other countries that would be of assistance to the United States.

"Hi, Tovarich"

With the new relationship initiated by former President Nixon between the People's Republic of China and the United States, countries throughout the world became much more interested in what exactly was going to happen on the world scene. One of the first to try to determine that was, of course, the Soviet Union. Their Politburo decided that the best way to do this was to invite a delegation of its counterparts from Congress to Moscow to discuss what their plans were and to try to determine what the United States' and Red China's positions were.

A U.S. delegation was put together and in 1977 went to the Soviet Union for discussions. Upon arrival in Moscow, we were immediately taken to our hotel and informed of a meeting scheduled for the morning with members of the Politburo. In the morning, we went to a building in the Russian parliament complex of buildings to meet with our counterparts. We met in an ornately decorated building with sets after sets of stairs leading from the main entrance to a meeting room. Discussions initiated by the Soviets began regarding issues such as, "what happens now," "what are we doing," and "what are some of the United States' plans?" After an all-morning exchange on these topics, we broke for lunch.

Down all the stairs we went, and out the front door. One of our delegates was Senator Hubert Humphrey of Minnesota, who had served as vice president in the late 1960s. And, as all who knew Senator Humphrey appreciated, he was a habitual campaigner. Across the street from the main entrance, about twenty Russians had gathered to take in what Americans look like; there they stood, gawking.

Senator Humphrey was not going to allow gawking only. He immediately rushed across the street and spoke English to Russian gawkers, who understood none. He campaigned up and down the line, shaking hands and telling them who he was and what office he was running for. Their response was wonderment and total confusion as to what Humphrey was doing or talking about! After lunch, we went back into a continuation of the morning's discussions.

The next morning, we headed for Stalingrad to lay a wreath at a memorial cemetery on the outskirts of the city. Its entrance was a small building with walls that depicted all the events during the three years the people of Stalingrad were under attack by the Nazis; it was a most impressive picture history. Leaving that building, we walked down a long path to the site of the memorial itself. The cemetery was comprised of large berms on each side of the walkway where the hundreds of thousands of slain Stalingrad natives were buried. An honor guard of tall Russian soldiers marched down the path, leading the delegation to the memorial site for the laying of the wreath. Funeral music played throughout the cemetery. It was a most impressive cemetery.

We left the cemetery and visited a well-known repository of Russia's gold collection. That evening we attended a dinner hosted by Stalingrad's mayor.

Following dinner, we went back to our hotel. We went to the control room for our delegation, which happened to have a balcony that overlooked our square. Even though it was two o'clock in the morning, the summer season still allowed for enough light that we could see people milling about below. Senator James Pearson's wife, realizing that we would be in Russia during America's Fourth of July, had brought with her some sparklers. She passed them around to the delegation. So here overlooking the square sat a group of Americans, waving sparklers and singing *The Star Spangled Banner*, in the middle of Russia and at two o'clock in the morning. That, in and of itself, was quite a thing to behold.

Continuing on, in 1980, the Senate was taken over by the Republican Party and Howard Baker became the majority leader. He selected Howard Liebengood to be his sergeant-at-arms, and I was fortunate enough to be elected as the secretary of the Senate. Shortly after taking office, Senator Baker—still a member of the Joint Committee on Atomic Energy (as appointed by Senator Scott)—decided he would like to meet with the

International Atomic Energy Commission. He also accepted an invitation for a visit from Prime Minister Golda Meier of Israel.

Prior to departing, we got word that President-elect Reagan was coming to the Hill to meet the leadership. Liebengood, newly elected sergeant-at-arms, became the official greeter to all dignitaries who visited the Capitol. He was concerned, however, as to how to address the president-elect. He went to Nordy Hoffman, the outgoing sergeant-at-arms, and asked him what to do. Nordy said, "Don't worry, just follow my lead."

With that, they left for the Senate entrance to the Capitol to greet Reagan. An entourage arrived, a limo door opened, and the president-elect stepped out. He was greeted by Nordy's, "Hi ya, Gipper!" as only a former Notre Dame football player could do! This left poor Liebengood speechless. Few presidents, if any, would have accepted graciously being called by their nickname by the sergeant-at-arms of the Senate—such graciousness was one of the things that made Reagan's term of office delightful, not only for the members of Congress, but also for the staff who had to deal with his people. (And of course his wife, Nancy, became the darling of all the Senate wives.) He was a complete gentleman, never got excited, and never seemed to get out of sorts. If you had to draw a picture of the perfect president in all ways, he would be it.

Still prior to our trip, Liebengood—who had not been on any of the so-called "Codels," short for "Congressional delegations"—came to me and asked exactly what he should do and how he should conduct himself on the trip. I told him not to worry about it, and he should just follow my lead and do pretty much whatever I did. And so we took off for our first stop in Copenhagen, Denmark.

Those were my "imbibing" days, which meant that by the time I arrived in Copenhagen, I was feeling very little pain. Traditionally on these trips, once we arrive in the host country, we go to a headquarters hotel where we meet the embassy representatives and receive our per diem (daily in-country expenditure allotment) for the stay. Once in Denmark, I went to the control room to receive my per diem, but I wasn't in any great shape to stand and sign for it. So, in my brilliance, I got down on my hands and knees next to the coffee table where I was able to sign my name, legibly or not. I looked around, and all of sudden over on the other side of the table, on his hands and knees also, was Liebengood, signing for his per diem, too. He was doing what I told him to do: follow my lead. It's a good thing I didn't decide to go out the window.

We went out that evening and did some sightseeing, and the next morning we headed to Brussels to meet with the secretary general of the International Atomic Energy Commission. We managed to find our way to the airport, board our plane, and, upon landing in Brussels, we were taken to the hotel for the meeting. Needless to say, neither Liebengood nor I were feeling anything by that time.

At the meeting room, staff sat along the back wall on benches, and the members sat in front. While the secretary general made his remarks, Liebengood fell asleep and began to snore. Sitting next to him was a lieutenant colonel in our delegation, who jabbed him to wake him up. But, the colonel jabbed Liebengood a little too hard and knocked him off the bench. Here, in the middle of this most important speech, Howard Liebengood is on the floor after having made quite a bit of noise with his fall. Much later, we laughed about that incident, and have laughed about it many times since.

Our next stop was Israel, where we had breakfast with Golda Meier. On this leg of the trip, there was still much imbibing going on, and when we went to breakfast, Senator Baker looked around and asked, "Where's Howard?" Another staff member offered to find him. Upon her return, she said, "Howard says that he's on the phone with State," which Baker took to mean the State Department. It turned out that the staff member had reported an interpretation of Howard's actual words, which were, "I'm on the floor in quite a state." That also brought much laughter, then and in many times to come.

How many rubles?

Entrance to Stalingrad Memorial Cemetery.

Honoring the Stalingrad dead.

The Stalingrad Survivor Monument.

Saw Ships Going Both Ways

Former presidents Ford and Nixon had been in favor of the Panama Canal Treaty and had offered it during their presidencies. However, Ronald Reagan, who was not yet president but was the choice of the convention in 1980, was opposed to the treaty. As a result, conservatives nationwide were also opposed to the treaty. Simply stated, Reagan and other conservatives were fearful of losing political, economic, and military control of this vital passageway. With a large number of Republicans in the Senate, this created a small problem for Senator Baker, for he thought that he would support the treaty. Thus, he did not feel comfortable with being the leader of the party, and therefore being expected to spearhead the opposition to the treaty.

Baker decided that in order to make sure that the conservatives felt that they had been dealt a fair hand, he went to Reagan's very close friend, Senator Paul Laxalt, and asked him if he would assume the leadership role for the debate on the treaty. Laxalt immediately said that he would be glad to do that. So, Laxalt would take the duty to argue against the treaty, and a possible conflict of interests was avoided.

In support of his position about the treaty, Senator Baker thought that it would be advantageous to go to Panama and meet with General Omar Torrijos, which he did. When he returned, he said that he was impressed by the general and that he had spoken with a number of Americans who were in the Canal Zone. His overall impression was that he felt that this was good for the country. He subsequently announced that he would support the treaty.

(A lesser member of the returning delegation held a press conference to elaborate important points about the trip and remark about the impressive canal where he had seen "ships going both ways!")

Meanwhile, Senator Robert Byrd, also indicating treaty support, stated his desire to meet with General Torrijos. He gathered six Democrats and they took off for Panama City to meet with the general and to talk to the Americans stationed in the zone.

At one point during the visit, Senator Byrd and the delegation were invited to have dinner with President Aristides Royo, a graduate of Texas A&M University. There was an overhead balcony at the dinner, from which musicians were entertaining. Senator Byrd, being from West Virginia, was much familiar with "Turkey in the Straw" as one of his fiddle pieces, so he wondered aloud to Royo whether he could join the musicians for some real down-home music. Royo thought that was a good idea, and Senator Byrd was on the music balcony pronto. To this day, it may be the only Panamanian rendition of "Turkey in the Straw" ever performed before a live audience.

Back in Washington, Senator Byrd and Senator Baker agreed that it would be beneficial for a delegation to travel through South America to get input from the leaders of various other countries and learn whether they supported transfer of the canal. Senator Byrd named Senator Ernest Hollings of South Carolina to lead that delegation, which left on a journey beginning with a stop in Rio de Janeiro. The group met with the powers that be in Rio and had a dinner party, which yours truly attended.

Following the dinner, which included just a few dinner drinks, I returned to the hotel (the Othon Palace) and proceeded to go to bed. However, during the night I dreamed that Senator Hollings had called a meeting at which I was expected to be present. Without any hesitation, I got up from the bed and went out the door to attend this meeting, only to find that the door had locked behind me; I had no key, was in my skivvies, and did not speak Portuguese. A hotel security detail approached me, quite concerned as to what I might be doing on that floor, in that hall, appearing as I did. I had difficulty explaining it to them since they did not understand English. The security chief decided to straighten this mystery out by taking me to the front desk to question a clerk on duty. The clerk recognized that I was part of the delegation, and so informed the security chief. Needless to say, that was another one of those embarrassing moments.

We left Rio de Janeiro for Brasilia to speak to the head of the Brazilian nation. Brasilia is not a well-known capital city. It is located some five hundred miles from Rio de Janeiro and has nothing of interest near it; its claim to importance is that all delegations from other countries do business there.

Our next stop was Chile, which was led by the dictator, Pinochet. He had agreed to see us and we were ushered into a room with a large conference table. In came Pinochet, dressed in army fatigues with two .45 caliber pistols strapped to his waist. He sat down and we began to discuss the treaty. Seemingly off task, one member of our delegation wasn't in any mood to discuss the treaty. He wanted to harangue Pinochet for being a dictator and utilizing heinous repression against Chile's citizens following his overthrow of democratically elected President Salvador Allende. We were aghast at the intensity of the accusations being levied. There was some question as to whether or not Pinochet would be offended to the point that we might not necessarily get out of there with our skins intact!

From there, we visited Peru, where we collected yet more affirmations for moving ahead with the treaty. No one we had visited was strongly opposed to us entering into the treaty to return the canal to the Panamanians.

Our last stop was Caracas, Venezuela. When we arrived at the train station, we met with a few dignitaries on a small platform where the chairmen of each delegation made some remarks. One of our senators was not quite sure what city he was in. He did know that he was in a foreign country because that was the purpose of the visit. As he got up to speak, he looked around and saw on the wall of the building the word "Cinzano," so he decided that that must be where he was! Taking the microphone, he greeted the dignitaries with his exclamations about how happy he was to be in a town as lovely as Cinzano! That pretty much spelled the end of the trip.

Upon our return to Washington, Senator Hollings reported that there was no significant dissension from the South American countries to the proposed treaty. Senator Laxalt was leading the opposition to the treaty and one of the members, Senator Brooke of Massachusetts, had an amendment that he wished to make to the Byrd-Baker amendment, which was to be the cornerstone of the treaty. He wondered whether or not the leadership would accept the language of his amendment. Negotiations required that all proposed amendments be transmitted to General Torrijos for his approval or disapproval; Torrijos had no objections to the Brooke amendment. Brooke was prepared to support the treaty if the language in his amendment was included, which it was. Shortly thereafter, the Senate voted in favor of the Panama Canal Treaty, and the United States turned possession of the canal over to the Panamanians.

A-shopping We Won't Go

In 1981, an interesting situation came up regarding Senator Mark Hatfield of Oregon. Or rather, the situation really involved his wife. Senator Hatfield, who had become chairman of the Appropriations Committee, felt that someone should be visiting the South Pole since there would be a line item for appropriating monies to the Pole, and yet the Senate did not know anything about the operations going on there. So, the senator put together a small group to visit. That meant flying into Christchurch, New Zealand, and then getting transportation from there to the South Pole. He also decided that just the senators would go to the Pole, while I and the rest of the delegation would go to Wellington and meet the senators at a later time.

After we arrived in Wellington and talked with our embassy staff, we were informed that the ambassador expected to have a small get-together at his home upon the senators' return. At the reception, I heard one embassy staff member talking with Mrs. Hatfield about a small town on the way to the airport that had a very delightful shopping street. Knowing that we had a meeting the next day in Australia and that if Mrs. Hatfield ever got the bus stopped in that small town we would still be there in mid afternoon, I asked one of the ambassador's aides if there was any way he could have the merchants delay opening in the morning until our bus passed en route to the airport. He said he would check and see.

I did not hear anything more about it, and the next morning we were on our way. When we got to the little town, Mrs. Hatfield instructed the driver to turn into the shopping area. We started down a street with lots of shops and noticed a window sign that said "closed." The next store had the same sign, and, in fact, each store on each side of the street had a closed sign in its window. I apologized to Mrs. Hatfield, saying I was so sorry that the stores were closed. We left the little town, got to the airport, and arrived in Australia in time for our meeting. Many years later, I told Mrs. Hatfield what I had done. Fortunately, she was amused, and I was allowed to finish my Senate career.

USAF—No Dogs

Delegations returning to the United States from European countries almost always go through London, as we did once on a trip from the Soviet Union. One of our staff regularly raised and showed Papillons. She heard that there was a breeder just outside London, so she visited and purchased an adorable three-year-old, planning to take it home. However, she soon learned that no animals were allowed on military airplanes. She appealed her case to the delegation chairman, but to no avail, so she arranged to have the embassy staff care for the pup until she could send for her. So as we departed down the runway, all eyes were on the sad sight of little "Codel," newly named, sitting on the runway as the plane took off. Some tears were shed and some said Codel waved good-bye. Believe it if you wish, but know that Codel is with her mistress and you can stop sobbing. Vaya con Dios.

Fly China Airlines or Walk

If you remember the earlier story about the Mansfield-Scott delegation trip to China, recall that our plane was sent out of the country, and we had to use China Airlines for our travels within the country. Some years later, Senator Thad Cochran, Republican from Mississippi, talked to the Republican party leader about taking a delegation to China to try to learn how the new policy of openness with America would affect our trade possibilities. The leader agreed, and a small delegation was put together to make the trip.

One of the members was Senator Paula Hawkins, Republican from Florida. Her interest was new markets for Florida oranges. She was a tigress, and gave the Chinese trade reps fits. But, we had another small problem—the head of the Chinese delegation notified us that we could not take our Air Force plane on in-country visits. We were not prepared to walk, so the Chinese provided a solution and asked to meet the delegation chairman. Senator Cochran asked me to go to the meeting and try to resolve the issue.

At the meeting, the Chinese revealed their solution: unpack our plane and transfer the personal luggage, control room, and food supplies onto a China Airlines plane and go on to Shanghai for the meeting. I was nonplused. First, I was a guest of the Chinese government; second, I was of no influential status. But, I did know that we were not going to turn into a van line. So I informed the Chinese negotiator that their solution was not acceptable and explained why. He said that he was sorry, but policy was policy. I had gotten some courage by then (I think from the Chinese tea) and replied that we, too, have a policy. Simply put, "Go with the guy that brought you, or don't go." I'm not sure they understood thoroughly, but they did indeed latch on to the "don't go" part. We were soon told to forget the policy and take our own plane. I informed the chairman, and he in his gentlemanly manner simply said okay. We believe it was the first time a U.S. Air Force plane was allowed to stay in-country during a visit.

What do you mean, walk home?

The Truth Squad—Campaign
Travel on a Shoestring

One more travel story I think you will enjoy is about political campaigning. It's 1964, and President Johnson is running for reelection against Mr. Conservative, Senator Barry Goldwater from Arizona. Somebody at the GOP headquarters decided we should have a "truth squad" follow the president around the country and correct what we believed would be his misstatements. Suddenly, President Johnson announced that he would make very few campaign trips, and would instead stay in the White House doing the country's business; however, the very loquacious Vice President Hubert Humphrey would carry the administration's banner.

We needed a magic carpet to carry us on our mission. At about that time, a supporter of Goldwater—a Mr. duPont from Florida—offered his plane for the truth squad's mission. So off we went like a bunch of Sinbads. Humphrey's first foray was a trip to visit Illinois, Oklahoma, and California, though not necessarily in that order. The truth squad flew to Los Angeles to await the vice president. He arrived and spoke at a Democratic rally in downtown LA, and we answered on a late night radio program.

Back at the hotel, cochairmen Carl Curtis of Nebraska and Congressman Bob Michel of Illinois gave us the bad news that we were broke, but due in Oklahoma the next day. Fortunately, we were in the land of Mr. Knottsbury, a Goldwater Republican whom Senator Curtis knew, and thus we managed to hit him up for a loan. Solvent again, we prepared to leave shortly after noon.

We had also added another member to our squad, Senator Milward Simpson of Wyoming. The senator mused that Mr. duPont had loaned a plane with not enough gas to get us there and back—do you think he thought we were going to taxi on Route 66? Anyhow, we left for Oklahoma and arrived in time for us to watch Governor Ronald Reagan of California make his Sunday night speech supporting the senator from Arizona. Humphrey could hardly wait for the "on air" light to go off before he was on TV dissecting the remarks, and of course we were right behind him.

It was off to Michigan the next day, and we had a late evening arrival in Traverse City. The Republican faithful met us with plans in place for a late television program schedule. We had a 6:00 AM departure in the morning heading for Illinois; dawn came much too early. Senator Simpson arrived, and when he reached the top of the airplane stairs, he turned and stared back at Traverse City and proclaimed, "Sure doesn't take long to spend a night in that town."

Our magic carpet was now folded away; the travel bureau closed. On to more serious business.

Qualities of Leadership

When there were things that the party leader or whip were responsible for, such as working out an agreement on which way to vote on a given piece of legislation, Senator Byrd would call for the proponents and opponents and together go at it hammer and tongue until they reached an agreement. Byrd would then go on the floor and announce the decision.

Prior to his leadership days, there were no "time agreements," which set limits on the hours of debate about a piece of pending legislation. We would just call it up and perhaps still be on it the next day. But time agreements served as heads-up to everyone. Senator Strom Thurmond (elected in 1954, turned one hundred-years-old just before he retired from the Senate in 2002 and died the following year), set the new filibuster record for speaking on the floor for twenty-four hours without ever yielding. After that, from time to time, members who didn't like a particular piece of legislation would use that ploy to keep a vote from being called. And if the issue was objectionable to many, they would take it up and talk for another day. But Byrd changed all that by getting a hundred senators to agree to time agreements.

When Lyndon Johnson was Senate majority leader, he was a tough taskmaster and riled up his own troops on numerous occasions. He demanded support for administration policy objectives, to be present for floor votes, and self-restraint for use of floor time. On one occasion, Senator Joe Clark of Pennsylvania had had enough of the taskmaster, and took to the Senate floor to voice his displeasure with the leader. While Clark's tirade went on, Mr. Bobby Baker, floor assistant to the leader, stood in the back of the chamber listening. After just so long he went to Johnson and said, "You can't let him speak like that about you without retribution."

"You're right," Johnson replied, "when he finishes, tell him I want to see him right away." Bobby Baker dutifully complied and handed Clark a note. Upon concluding his remarks, he immediately went to see the leader.

The majority leader's desk sits in the front of the chamber in full view of the press and public galleries. Their talk became quite animated, with swinging of arms and face-to-face confrontation. Finally, Clark threw up his hands and stomped out of the chamber; Johnson immediately gestured to Baker to come see him. Senator Johnson glared at Mr. Baker and exclaimed, "Well, since you're so smart and since he told me to go to hell, now what do I do?" Mr. Baker scurried up the center aisle and out the doors. Johnson was such a strong leader that this did not faze him, and he went back to doing what he had been doing. So much for the leaders.

Sometimes seeing the lackluster intellectuality of some of the members of the Senate is a head-shaker. On one occasion, my assistant and I were preparing an explanation of what the leader's position would be on an amendment that was then under discussion. This exercise was to inform members as they arrived to vote. One afternoon, we were approached by a senator inquiring what time we expected a vote to occur, and we advised him it would be at about four o'clock. "Good," he said, "I can go for a jog and still make the vote," and off he went.

Sure enough, the warning bell rang for a four o'clock vote. The leadership allows members twenty minutes to get to the floor before calling it off. This allowance was about up when the doors flew open and in the doorway stood our jogger calling for recognition, but not dressed in the uniform of the day. Later we learned that he had changed into jogging garb in a Senate office building. When he heard that the vote was called, he dutifully went to change clothes again in order to make the vote. One small problem—he couldn't remember which building or which men's room his dress clothes were in. Does that make your head shake?

One has to look very carefully to find emerging statesmen among today's legislators. The Ohio Republican Party had already elected two U.S. senators (from the political Taft family) and had claim to fame for one U.S. attorney general, former Senator Bill Saxbe. All were strict conservatives. Then Ohio elected a senator whom they thought was a fiscal conservative, but Democrats are never fiscal conservatives, and this man was true to form. One day following passage of a bill that increased each senator's office staff salaries (provided that a senator *agreed to grant* them to his staff), Ohio democratic senator, Howard Metzenbaum, stated on the floor that not one of his staff was worthy of the raise. At that time, unfortunately for him, we had open communications between the offices and the floor, which meant that his staff heard all that he said. When he went to his office, he couldn't get in, because the doors were locked and no one was there. He wondered what had happened! Eventually he had to call everyone, promise the increases, and request that they please come back to work. But that behavior is not statesmanlike—that was Howard Metzenbaum.

Today, the old school of honor is still represented by Senator Thad Cochran as well as Senator Byrd, but then the list gets thin. The elder statesmen got elected because they were well-known in their states, perhaps by having been governor or attorney general, or having held other well-respected positions. Now the electorate is offered someone who is endorsed by some commercial interest group, like bankers or insurance, and they spread a lot of ads telling about the greatness of the man until people eventually believe it and he gets elected. In the book I talk a little about party conventions as a better way to get statesmen not beauty queens. To some, party conventions won't make a more responsive Senate. But it's worth thinking about; the present method doesn't seem to be working.

Voice

In the some twenty-five years that I served the Congress, I was privileged to work under or know five Senate Leaders, beginning with Everett McKinley Dirksen from Pekin, Illinois. Senator Dirksen was a strong conservative and was an excellent leader for the Republican senators.

A quality that Senator Dirksen had going for him was a beautiful and compelling voice that drew everyone to be present when he spoke on the floor. If the word went out that Senator Dirksen was about to speak, various Senate buildings' office doors flew open like at a Macy's sale, and staff poured out of them to get to the Capitol to hear him speak. Since all staff had floor privileges, they got on the little train that took them to Capitol—we should have had more cars.

In those days, we had leather couches in the back of the chamber, but staff members were permitted to sit on the floor in front of those couches; so there they sat. When Senator Dirksen completed his remarks, there was the feeling among staff that they wanted to cry, "Encore! Encore!" But had they done so, they would have immediately been thrown off the floor and probably not had their passes returned to them. Senator Dirksen was that kind of a speaker; not only was his message important, but his delivery was much more important. He was an excellent leader, as I've indicated, and had been a close friend of President Johnson's when he was the Democratic leader in the Senate.

Following President Kennedy's untimely death and Vice President Johnson's becoming president, there were times that President Johnson might call Senator Dirksen's office and say, "Ev, I'm coming up." In a short time, and with his beagle in tow, LBJ would show up, and he and Dirksen would discuss whatever they had to discuss and have a small scotch. (Some of the more conservative senators were not comfortable with their leader sipping schnapps with the president, but truth be known, he learned more to help Republicans than he would have at a White House meeting.) Johnson and Dirksen had crossed swords for years on party issues, but they both had successfully led their parties through many difficult times. Johnson realized how much of a problem it was for Dirksen to lose someone of Kuchel's caliber and to get him replaced as whip; he knew what he was going through.

Senator Dirksen prided himself in running a well-organized minority with no dissenters. This wasn't one of those times. He wasted little time in notifying his troops that Senator Roman Hruska was his choice as the next whip. No need for a contest. However, Senator Dirksen failed to recognize that changes had occurred among his troops; some of the conservative senators had served long enough to begin thinking about leadership positions for themselves. As recounted early in this book, they quietly rebelled against the leader and voted for Pennsylvanian Hugh Scott, much to the consternation of the Senator from Pekin. With the Senate Republican numbers, they stacked their hopes on being able to defeat Senator Scott if he decided to go for leader. They were probably right, for it was a different Republican minority than it is now, much more cohesive.

"How-To" Manual

When Scott was the Republican leader, the Democrats had Senator Mike Mansfield of Montana as their leader, and he and Senator Scott got along famously. In fact, they and their wives made the trip to China following Nixon's visit, as discussed previously. Shortly after Scott's election, Mansfield stopped by his office, much to the consternation of the receptionist, who was speechless. Finally, Mansfield said, "Is he in?" which really was all he ever said. The receptionist regained her voice, so no harm done. Scott, on occasion, would telephone Mansfield's office to see if he was available and go around the corner to see him.

In 1976, both Senator Mansfield and Senator Scott decided to resign their seats. So, as we went into the latter years of the Carter administration, the Senate had lost its two leaders. On the Democratic side, Senator Robert Byrd, who had been Senator Mansfield's whip, became the Democratic leader, and Howard Baker became—finally, after three tries—the Republican leader. Senator Byrd, of Panama fame, was a man of the Senate. The Senate was his love, and he had an idea of how he thought the Senate (and, more importantly, its members) should conduct themselves.

One of the major problems was the members, and particularly their wives, not knowing how long each session would be. The length of the sessions was important, particularly for wives who had to prepare dinner. They were as vocal as their husbands about trying to bring some order to the method of the Senate's operation. So Senator Byrd came up with a solution, which has lasted for as long as the Senate. Byrd's solution was to simply, by unanimous consent, obtain time limits on the legislation and amendments to be discussed. This meant that before the leadership ever took up a bill on the floor, they had a time agreement in place for not only the bill, but amendments thereto. It greatly aided the senators, their staffs, and their families in being aware of exactly how long the Senate debate was going to take. Plus, it would have taken unanimous consent to have changed any of these time agreements, because they had been arrived at by unanimous agreement.

Byrd not only changed the operation of the Senate, but he made a series of speeches on the history of the Senate, which is in the Congressional Record. He also had a good relationship with Senator Baker, even though their political philosophies were different. But he would not take any actions detrimental to the Republican Party without consulting with Senator Baker beforehand. And Baker would likewise consult with Senator Byrd. In attempting to analyze the effectiveness of those leaders, it had to be remembered that they served under differing administrations, so each individual's effectiveness was different and the things that they had to do were different. So the conclusion, from my standpoint, can be made that each of them was as effective as they could be during their service, and I could not judge which of them might be considered the better leader.

The one thing that this points out is the difference between then and now. Today's Senate leadership almost never talks to each other and there is very little communication. They are advocates, rather than friends. It is not a pleasant place to be at this time, and as a result, the Senate is no longer the effective body that it was back in those days. I have said many times that in many states, politicians have replaced the statesmen who served back in those days.

These are my thoughts on the Senate leadership and the difference between then and now. The previous leaders, almost without exception, put the Senate and its operation as a number-one consideration for their leadership. Today, there is no love of the Senate as an institution. The members treat their participation as a United States Senator as they would if they were in a nine-to-five private sector job.

Their actions as legislators may leave much to be desired, but I don't think it is with malice or forethought. So, while this behavior may be critical of the existing leadership, it may only be a reflection of the differing times. Part of those differing times is the total lack of interest by citizens about what is happening in the legislature and what the requirements should be to serve in the Congress. Citizens today seem to be driven only by personal issues that are direct concerns of theirs. So, if they proceed to vote based on that assumption, then the overall expertise of former senators and leaders will be totally lacking. As a result, the public is electing the single-issue-minded people that the electorate had in mind in sending them to Washington.

My twenty-five years of service allow me to judge what happens in the Senate today. What has happened is the senators have become single-issue advocates. In prior years, senators got elected for their positions on subjects crucial to their constituencies. In fact, sometimes you could get elected by the senate leadership committing to place you on a certain committee of responsibility that included an issue critical to your constituents. Now politicians run on the leading issue, nationwide as well as statewide—issues that many times they won't even have a chance to vote on. My advice to the voters is as follows: return elections to the state parties and get rid of the beauty pageants; elect the most competent, not the prettiest. The members should act like graduating seniors, not preschoolers. At least no male senator has put his female colleague's pigtail in the inkwell, which, by the way, is on every chamber desk.

Surprise! Surprise!

One of the more interesting challenges of being on the leadership floor staff is trying to predict how senators may vote. A case in point occurred in early 1970 when President Nixon sent up the administration's voting rights proposal. As is customary, a member of the president's party introduces the proposal, which is then referred to the appropriate committee—in this case the Senate Judiciary Committee, which included Senator Phil Hart of Michigan, Senator Scott of Pennsylvania, and Senator Hruska of Nebraska. The bill, as you might imagine, was far from what Hart and Scott wanted in a bill of this importance, so they drafted a stronger version that became the bill reported from the committee for floor consideration. Upon introduction, the debate took off.

During the debate, Mr. Conservative, Arizona's Senator Barry Goldwater, came by Scott's leader office to show him an amendment on relaxing the requirements on members of the armed services and other government employees. Goldwater wondered if Senators Scott and Hart could accept the amendment and add it to the bill, as it was obvious by this time that this bill would pass. Scott and Hart immediately told Goldwater to bring it to the floor and offer it, and they would accept it—which he did, and the senator's amendment became part of the bill.

The debate had droned on long enough for Senator Hruska, who was managing the opposition to the bill. He walked into Scott's office and informed him that he was preparing to move to table the bill, a maneuver which, if carried, would effectively kill it. Scott and Hart said fine and thanked Hruska for the heads-up. The senator went on the floor and moved to table the pending legislation. The clerk began to call the roll, and most Republicans were voting yes to kill the bill. The clerk got down to the Gs and said, "Mr. Goldwater," and Barry said an emphatic *no*. With that, Senator Hruska almost went through the Capitol dome and rushed across the Senate floor to talk to Goldwater and tell him that the vote was a *yes* vote.

"Not for me," retorted Goldwater. "I have an amendment in that bill, and I sure as hell am not going to vote to kill my own bill."

I hope this anecdote points out the importance of knowing what's in the legislation and how you should vote. Senator Hruska and his staff missed the fact that Goldwater had offered an amendment, had it adopted, and it was part of the bill. Had Hruska known this before the vote, he could have talked to Goldwater and made him a deal: "If you vote to table, I will assure you that your amendment will be in the administration's bill when it comes before the Senate."

Goldwater was a veteran legislator and knew full well that the Scott-Hart version would be the only bill to pass this Senate. Had he accepted Hruska's offer, he would be amending a bill that already had "death rattles." I cite this for the readers to give them a feel for the behind-the-scenes goings-on in the Senate. These were the days when members spoke to each other, visited each other's offices, and tried to work out sticky problems. There was great respect for each other, and they realized their charter from the voters. Today, it is reminiscent of a schoolyard ball game where, "If you don't play by my rules, I take the ball home and the game is over." Readers: too many balls have been taken home.

Top Dogs?

Throughout this book, I have mentioned various leadership races and eventual party leaders. There is quite a difference between the minority leader and the majority leader. On the one hand, the minority leader's party and that of the president may be the same. If the majority of Congress does not share the president's party affiliation, then the minority leader's position becomes not as difficult as that of the majority leader, because the minority leader is only responsible for the votes of the members of his own party—while the majority leader must at least hold onto all of his members' votes. That disparity causes some interesting scenarios, such as when the president sends legislation to construct a fence along the border between Mexico and the United States. He charges the minority leader with the job of securing enough votes to enact the legislation (of course, when pigs fly). Now comes the big difference between being a minority or majority leader. A minority leader is responsible for securing enough votes to pass proposed legislation. A majority leader just needs enough to defeat it, which, by definition of majority, should not be very difficult. The bottom line is that, as minority leader with the same party affiliation as the president, the work is actually on his behalf and accomplished by doing his bidding. Most well-respected minority leaders accept this role and attempt to rise to its challenges.

Sometimes the White House gets brain-dead, can't count, and gets too heavy-handed. One time, presidential aide John Ehrlichman asked to meet with Senator Scott and then-Congressman Gerald Ford to discuss an administration proposal that had as much attractiveness to the president's party as ants at a picnic. Scott and Ford talked before the meeting and agreed that this was a nonstarter. Ehrlichman sat there and explained how much this proposal meant to the president. Both Ford and Scott said too bad, *no way*. Ehrlichman, with that smug smile, made a fatal error when he said that anyone who was to vote against this measure would see the president personally go to their district and support the opposition. Ford looked at Scott incredulously. They both smiled smiles that seemed to say, "Can we help him with his travel schedule?"

Nancy Who?

When the voters turned the legislative branch over to the Democrats and left the executive in Republican hands, it left the president with no one to introduce an administration proposal without possibly finding a sympathetic Democrat. Hey Nancy! (Pelosi.) Her line is busy, can you take a message? (Yeah, right.) Press one for English. Seriously, the result of your votes have cut the president's umbilical cord and left him an orphan. Where's Senator Baker when we need him?

I ask a favor of you, the voter, if you don't mind. Remain vigilant; don't turn your back on your congressional representatives. They are there to help; pray they do.

The Fox in Charge of the Chicken Coop

Voters were unhappy about the president but he wasn't seeking election, so they turned to whoever was. As a result, control of the legislative branch was given to the Democrats at a time when the Republicans were still in charge of the White House. "Gadzooks!" Not a pretty legislative picture. Speaker of the House Pelosi and Senate Majority Leader Harry Reid have the votes to pass anything, but not enough to override a presidential veto. The president can propose legislation to be introduced by Senate Minority Leader Mitch McConnell, but if Democrats don't like it, the proposed legislation will just languish until eventually forgotten. This is not necessarily good for the country.

Can anything be done?

Of course. Senator McConnell should walk up the hall to the majority leader's office and discuss the problem with him. Senator Reid just might say something like, "Hell, Mitch, I'll talk to the committee chairman, and maybe we can have some hearings." This makes the Republicans happy, the president and McConnell are happy, and McConnell can live to fight another day. If this were to happen, the Senate would be a pleasant place to be, and the constituents would get their money's worth with a productive senator looking out for them, rather than some special interest. Hooray! Our democracy is safe, and as long as they communicate with each other, the Republicans will have their own "Camelot."

To this day, there is still one member in the Senate who has always preached this philosophy of getting things done—Senator Robert Byrd of West Virginia. With Senator Mansfield's concurrence, Senator Byrd personalized the leader's office. He listened to members' complaints and solved them if he could. A case in point: when Republican members had a problem with the Easter recess dates, they came to Senator Scott and explained that they all had children in Washington DC schools, but lived in different districts with varying recess schedules. Senator Byrd recognized the problem and went about scheduling the recess at a time when the fewest members and their families would be negatively affected. He also used the same means to solve legislative problems.

Follow the Leader

I was present in the Senate during the Johnson, Dirksen, Mansfield, and Byrd leadership years. I was administrative assistant to Senator Scott when he was leader and, thanks to Senator Baker, was secretary of the Senate when he became leader in January 1981. What kind of a leader was Baker?

An intelligent and sensitive man, Baker knew well, for instance, the gracious handling he had received from Senator Scott during his earlier defeats in races for minority leader. Baker's grandmother had been an elected sheriff of a small rural Tennessee county. His father, Howard H. Baker, had been a congressman, whose seat upon his passing was filled by Baker's mother, Irene Bailey Baker. Furthermore, the contemporary Howard Baker had married the daughter of Senator Dirksen. Did we think he was going to be a bus driver? I don't think so. And if he was in the parade, he was going to lead it. So true to that ambition, eventually rumors surfaced that he might run against Scott for leader yet again. Senator Baker is alleged to have said, "I can't afford to run against him another time. I have no idea what the hell he would appoint me to if I lost again!"

Baker loved politics, as did the others in the Senate. On his first meeting with the rest of the leadership, he said that President Reagan wanted to raise the national debt, a fall-on-your-sword position to Republicans everywhere. Baker made the pitch for why this had to be done, and the first voice raised was that of South Carolina's senator, the late Strom Thurmond, who had never voted for raising the national debt in his life. But Thurmond said, "We follow the leader."

Baker's leadership qualities rose once again in tackling divisions over the issue of Tennessee's Constitution calling for "one man, one vote" in the state legislature or in representation in the U.S. Congress. This provision of law was dutifully (read: politically) opposed by the Senate Republican leader, Everett McKinley Dirksen, Baker's father-in-law. Without a by-your-leave, Senator Baker went to the floor in one of his earliest speeches and opposed his father-in-law's and his party's position on this issue. As the saying goes, "dance with the guy that brang you," which is what Baker did—"You sent me, I represent you." And so he did, and very well, putting country before politics.

And that's where Baker differed from other leaders who have since succeeded him. By going away from the personal respect and bipartisanship that permeated the Baker, Scott, Mansfield, and Byrd eras, the new Senate has done a disservice to the people and has led us to where we are today. To right this ship of state, we must find more statesmen. In summary, Baker was a leader's leader, and we might not see the likes of him again.

Howard Baker in the garden at the U.S. Embassy in Tokyo. Following his service in the Senate and as chief of staff to President Reagan, he was the U.S. Ambassador to Japan.

Time's A-here—Charge to Electorate

I would like you, the voting reader, to consider how you react to our current slipshod, unproductive legislature. I will confine my views to the Senate and ask you to consider the importance of your vote in the next election. To shed light on the importance of remaining vigilant about the political scene, and especially about who is seeking elective office, I reflect on a poem we all should know well:

> First they came for the Jews
> and I did not speak out
> because I was not a Jew.
> Then they came for the Communists
> and I did not speak out
> because I was not a Communist.
> Then they came for the trade unionists
> and I did not speak out
> because I was not a trade unionist.
> Then they came for me
> and there was no one left
> to speak out for me.
>   —*Pastor Martin Niemoller*

If you are concerned about the kind of a society that will be left for your children or grandchildren, it is as you wish if you don't become active in politics and take an active interest in the people who you are electing. If we remain complacent, there will be nobody left to help future generations. Please make politics as important to you as you do your children's health, and leave them a land as safe and as beautiful as was left for you.

The Return of Greatness

Before I bring a finish to this book, I should bring you up to date on the new Senate atmosphere permeating the chamber. I have been critical at times of the direction I thought the leaders from the late eighties until now were taking the Senate. The United States Senate has become one hundred individual men and women with few friendships and little, if any, comity. But a new mood has surfaced, led by the senator from Nevada, Majority Leader Harry Reid, and the senator from Kentucky, Minority Leader Mitch McConnell. No longer do the members have to go to their wives to find out if there is school tomorrow; the two leaders have copied the old "Ev & Charlie Show"—an Everett Dirksen-Charlie Halleck (Halleck was the Republican House minority leader at the time) television program designed to humanize the Senate and the House. Dirksen and Halleck would converse about the workings of the Congress for the television audience.

Now Reid and McConnell are meeting every Monday morning before the session starts so that they each know what's going to happen, and the troops will be told also. No more surprises—just sound, meaningful legislation.

I can hear Senator Mansfield and Senator Scott looking down and saying, "I never thought they would get it. But, they did." There's a light at the end of the tunnel. Now members can reach across the aisle and say, "Good to see you; by the way, I've got a bill I'd like you to look at."

The Founding Fathers said, "We gave you a Republic if you can keep it." *And we can.*

Epilogue

Some of you may not have heard the phrase "smoke-filled room"—or thought it might be a cigar or cigarette commercial—but that was not the case. The phrase was actually a media invention signifying something not quite right. In reality, when the phrase was coined, the local political machine had been taken over by the union officials, the prohibition opponents, and the gangsters. Political history is replete with stories about powerful machines controlling city and state governments, i.e., Tammany Hall. But the country was changing—suffering through a devastating depression and a World War that was costly in human life.

Suddenly, "politics" was no longer a dirty word; people began to realize that politics were going to control their lives and the lives of their children—hence strong open-door political parties—neighbor and neighbor, friend and friend, public servants and little people, with similar interests on such subjects as education, economy, and social needs. Along came satellite groups from the cities and the counties. "Let's have a state convention and limit the number of voting delegates and endorse a candidate for the Senate because he's competent and qualified to represent us," they said. "He might not be the most popular, but he's the most competent."

If you have the time, look at your two senators from sixty years ago and compare them to today's two. They were all honorable men but sixty years ago—you knew they represented you, and today you're not sure. This is not meant as an indictment of the one hundred honorable and well-meaning men and women who serve in the world's greatest deliberative body.

I hope that gives you a feel for the difference between party state conventions and today's run for the key to the U.S. Treasury. Sometime earlier in the book, somebody kicked over the soapbox, and I think they just did it again.

Vaya con Dios

About the Author

Outside of those elected to the Senate, few individuals have had a more intimate perspective of its workings than has Bill Hildenbrand. Senator Howard Baker said, "He is as close to the total Senate man as I've ever met."

Bill Hildenbrand's three decades on Capitol Hill began in 1957 as research assistant to Delaware's Republican U.S. representative, Harry G. Haskell. Four years later he joined the staff of Delaware's U.S. senator, J. Caleb Boggs. In 1967 he became administrative assistant to Hugh Scott of Pennsylvania, the Senate Republican whip, and continued in that capacity when Scott was elected majority leader in 1972. He won elections as secretary of the minority in 1975 and as the twenty-third secretary of the United States Senate in 1981.

Since retiring in 1985, Mr. Hildenbrand has lived with his wife, Shirley, in Vero Beach, Florida.

978-0-595-42709-3
0-595-42709-X

www.ingramcontent.com/pod-product-compliance
Lightning Source LLC
Chambersburg PA
CBHW030343290526
45785CB00004B/1581